How To Study:

EASY **I AM YOUR GRAMMAR**

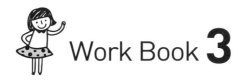

Work Book **3**

Iambooks

Contents

B

Chapter 1
Nouns, Pronouns and Adjectives

A[An] / The + Noun

Grammar focus

I have **a** pencil.

I have pencil**s**.

Look at **the** moon.

I see **an** elephant.
The elephant is big.

1. 명사의 복수형은 어떻게 만드나요?

❶ 대부분의 명사 뒤에 -s를 붙입니다. (books, apples)

❷ 〈자음＋y〉로 끝나는 명사는 -y를 없애고 -ies를 붙여요. (babies, cities)

❸ -s, -sh, -ch, -x, -o로 끝나는 명사는 -es를 붙여요. (buses, boxes, dishes, watches)

❹ -f(e)로 끝나는 명사는 -f(e)를 없애고 -ves를 붙여요. (knives, leaves, wolves)

❺ 규칙이 없는 복수형 명사들도 있어요.

foot – feet	man – men	fish – fish	child – children
tooth – teeth	woman – women	sheep – sheep	mouse – mice

2. 관사 a/an이 뭐예요?

a/an은 셀 수 있는 명사 앞에 붙어서 하나(의)라는 뜻을 가지고 있어요. a/an은 '한 개(하나)'의 의미이므로 복수명사, 고유명사, 그리고 셀 수 없는 명사의 앞에는 붙일 수 없어요.

3. 정관사 the는 언제 쓰는 건가요?

a/an은 정해지지 않은 명사 앞에 사용하고, the는 이미 앞에서 언급해서 서로 알고 있거나 세상에 단 하나밖에 없는 대상(자연) 앞에 써요.

the sun, **the** earth, **the** moon, **the** sky, **the** sea, **the** Statue of Liberty

I have **a** puppy. **The** puppy is very cute.

Go for it!

A. Look and circle the correct word.

1.

(a / (an)) umbrella

2.

(a / an) box

3.

(a / an) apple

4.

(a / an) puppy

5.

(a / an) girl

6.

(a / an) elephant

B. Write *a, an, the* or *X*.

1. _____X_____ women

2. _____ animal

3. _____ man

4. _____ children

5. _____ moon

6. _____ airplane

7. _____ earth

8. _____ sky

9. _____ feet

10. _____ orange

11. _____ angel

12. _____ ant

13. _____ teacher

14. _____ students

C. Write the plural form.

Singular	Plural	Singular	Plural
1. a book	books	2. a box	
3. a watch		4. a leaf	
5. a country		6. a child	
7. a woman		8. a man	
9. a baby		10. a dish	
11. a tooth		12. a foot	

D. Write *a, an* or *the.*

1. She is ___a___ happy girl. ___The___ girl is happy.

2. There is _____ dictionary on the desk.
   _____ dictionary is big and heavy.

3. I have _____ apple and _____ orange.

4. We see _____ eagle. It is flying in _____ sky.

5. There is _____ woman in the picture.
   _____ woman is wearing glasses.

Grammar in Writing

A. Fill in the blanks and rewrite the sentences into the plural form.

1. It is __*a*__ box. ➡ *They are boxes* _____.

2. It is _____ umbrella. ➡ _____.

3. It is _____ knife. ➡ _____.

4. It is _____ leaf. ➡ _____.

5. It is _____ puppy. ➡ _____.

6. It is _____ bench. ➡ _____.

B. Read and rewrite the sentences.

1. It is a green apple. ➡ *The apple is green* _____.

2. He is a brave soldier. ➡ _____.

3. It is delicious pizza. ➡ _____.

4. She is a famous doctor. ➡ _____.

5. It is a small bird. ➡ _____.

Pronouns

They are students.
That is **their** digital camera.
The digital camera is **theirs**.

This is Linda.
She is a tennis player.
The tennis racket is **hers**.

1. 대명사가 뭐예요?

대명사는 명사를 대신하는 말로 인칭대명사와 지시대명사가 있어요.

	단수(Singular)			복수(Plural)		
	주격	소유격	소유대명사	주격	소유격	주격대명사
1 인칭	I (나는)	my (나의)	mine (나의 것)	we (우리들은)	our (우리들의)	ours (우리들의 것)
2 인칭	you (너는)	your (너의)	yours (너의 것)	you (너희들은)	your (너희들의)	yours (너희들의 것)
3 인칭	he (그는)	his (그의)	his (그의 것)	they (그(것)들은)	their (그(것)들의)	theirs (그(것)들의 것)
	she (그녀는)	her (그녀의)	hers (그녀의 것)			
	it (그것은)	its (그것의)	X			

2. 지시대명사가 뭐예요?

지시대명사란 우리말에 이것(this), 저것(that)처럼 손가락으로 지시하듯이 가리키며 사용하는 말이에요.
공간적으로 가까이 있는 것을 가리키며 말할 때는 this(복수는 these), 공간적으로 또는 눈으로 보기에
조금 멀리 떨어져 있는 것을 가리킬 때는 that(복수는 those)를 써요.

A. Look and circle the correct word.

1.

(This / That) is a car.

2.

(These / Those) are oranges.

3.

(This / That) is a pig.

4.

(These / Those) are geese.

B. Look and fill in the blanks.

		주격	소유격	소유대명사
단수	1인칭	I	_____	_____
	2인칭	_____	your	_____
	3인칭	she	_____	_____
		he	_____	_____
복수	1인칭	we	_____	_____
	2인칭	_____	your	_____
	3인칭	they	_____	_____

C. Read and circle the correct word.

1. It is your pencil.
   → It is (your / (yours)).

2. It is their house.
   → It is (they / them / theirs).

3. It is my MP3 player.
   → It is (me / I / mine).

4. They are your shoes.
   → They are (you / your / yours).

5. It is our car.
   → It is (us / we / ours).

6. They are her rings.
   → They are (her / hers / she).

D. Read and complete the sentences.

1. This is my coat. The coat is ____mine____.

2. This is his book. The book is _____.

3. These are your sunglasses. The sunglasses are _____.

4. That cell phone is for Sunny. The cell phone is _____.

5. My flowers are over there. These flowers are _____.

6. These are his roller skates. The roller skates are _____.

7. These are our dolls. These dolls are _____.

8. These are their dictionaries. The dictionaries are _____.

Grammar in Writing

A. Read and complete the answers.

1. Q: Is this your book? (he)
   A: No, _____it isn't_____ . _____It is his_____ .

2. Q: Are these her sunglasses? (I)
   A: No, _____ . _____ .

3. Q: Is that his MP3 player? (she)
   A: No, _____ . _____ .

4. Q: Are these your piggy banks? (they)
   A: No, _____ . _____ .

5. Q: Is this their bicycle? (we)
   A: No, _____ . _____ .

B. Look and write.

1. (ant)
   Q: _____Is_____ _____this_____ an elephant?
   A: _No, it isn't_ . _It is an ant_ .

2. (ice-skates)
   Q: _____ _____ bikes?
   A: _____ . _____ .

3. (apple)
   Q: _____ _____ oranges?
   A: _____ . _____ .

4. (frog)
   Q: _____ _____ a puppy?
   A: _____ . _____ .

13

Grammar focus

There is **some** milk.
There is **some** bread.
Are there **any** apples?
No, there aren't **any** apples.

1. some과 any는 어떨 때 쓰는 건가요?

any는 some과 똑같이 '몇몇의, 약간(조금)'의 뜻으로 그 수나 양을 정확히 모를 때 사용하는 말이에요.

2. some과 any는 쓰임이 같은가요?

some은 긍정문에 쓰고, any는 주로 부정문과 의문문에 써요. 둘 다 셀 수 있는 명사나 셀 수 없는 명사 앞에 모두 쓸 수 있어요.

some + noun	Affirmatives (긍정문)	There are some pencils. Tom has some juice.
any + noun	Negatives (부정문)	There aren't any pencils. Tom doesn't have any juice.
	Questions (의문문)	Are there any pencils? Does Tom have any juice?

Usage

Kevin has **some** milk.
He doesn't have **any** coffee.
Does he have **any** water?
No, he doesn't.

There are **some** books.
There aren't **any** erasers.
Are there **any** toys?
No, there aren't.

Go for it!

A. Look and cirlce the correct word.

1. (a / (some)) water   2. (an / some) orange juice

3. (a / some) cups   4. (a / some) book

5. (a / some) fruit   6. (an / some) umbrella

7. (a / some) ball   8. (a / some) salt

9. (a / some) milk   10. (a / some) knives

B. Read and circle the correct word.

1. There aren't (some / (any)) windows in this room.

2. I have (some / any) magazines.

3. Is there (some / any) milk in the refrigerator?

4. There isn't (some / any) orange juice.

5. They eat (some / any) ice creams for dessert.

6. Do you need (some / any) money?

7. Nancy doesn't have (some / any) puppies.

8. There are (some / any) children in the classroom.

C. Write <some/any+noun>.

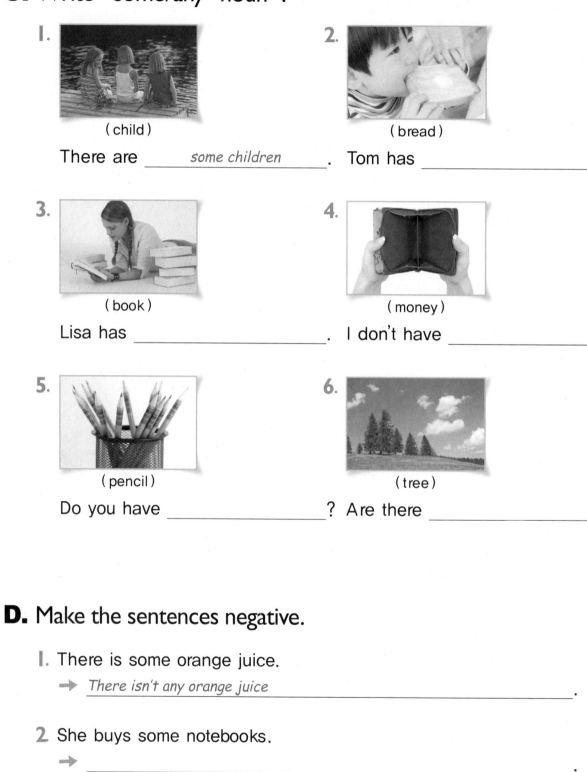

1.

(child)

There are _____some children_____ .

2.

(bread)

Tom has _____ .

3.

(book)

Lisa has _____ .

4.

(money)

I don't have _____ .

5.

(pencil)

Do you have _____ ?

6.

(tree)

Are there _____ ?

D. Make the sentences negative.

1. There is some orange juice.

   ➡ _There isn't any orange juice_ _____ .

2. She buys some notebooks.

   ➡ _____ .

3. There are some flowers.

   ➡ _____ .

Grammar in Writing

A. Read and make answers.

1. Q: Does she drink any milk? (orange juice)
   A: No, _____she doesn't_____ . _____She drinks some orange juice_____ .

2. Q: Are there any books on the desk? (pencils)
   A: No, _____ . _____ .

3. Q: Does he have any caps? (bags)
   A: No, _____ . _____ .

4. Q: Does she have any salt? (cheese)
   A: No, _____ . _____ .

5. Q: Is there any water in the bottle? (milk)
   A: No, _____ . _____ .

B. Look at the pictures and complete the sentences using *some* or *any*.

1.

   Susan has _____some goldfish_____ .
   She doesn't have _____any hamsters_____ .

   goldfish (O) / hamster (X)

2.

   Bob has _____ .
   He doesn't have _____ .

   egg (O) / apple (X)

3.

   Kathy has _____ .
   She doesn't have _____ .

   milk (O) / coffee (X)

unit 4 many / much / a lot of

Grammar focus

many eggs

much snow

a lot of cars

a lot of money

1. many와 much는 뭐예요?

'많은'이라는 의미로 특별히 정해지지 않은 수나 양을 나타낼 때 써요. many는 셀 수 있는 명사 앞, much는 셀 수 없는 명사 앞에 오며, much는 특히 부정문과 의문문에 주로 써요.

2. a lot of는 뭐예요?

똑같이 '많은'의 뜻으로 셀 수 있는 명사와 셀 수 없는 명사 앞에 모두 쓸 수 있어요. many나 much 대신에 a lot of를 써도 같은 뜻이 되는 거예요.

many + countable nouns(셀 수 있는 명사)	many books, many students
much + uncountable nouns(셀 수 없는 명사)	much snow, much bread, much water
a lot of + countable/uncountable nouns	a lot of pencils, a lot of cheese

Usage

There is **much** water.
(=a lot of)

There are **many** people.
(=a lot of)

There are **a lot of** books.
(=many)

Go for it!

A. Choose and write.

1.

She has ___*a lot of*___ books.

(much / (a lot of))

2.

Bob has _____ car.

(much / a)

3.

Nancy drinks _____ coffee.

(much / many)

4.

I have _____ friends.

(much / a lot of)

5.

We need _____ money.

(a lot of / many)

6.

There are _____ penguins.

(many / much)

B. Circle all the correct answers.

1. (**many** / much / **a lot of**) oranges
2. (many / much / a lot of) cheese
3. (many / much / a lot of) water
4. (many / much / a lot of) milk
5. (many / much / a lot of) ants
6. (many / much / a lot of) flowers
7. (many / much / a lot of) trees
8. (many / much / a lot of) butter
9. (many / much / a lot of) juice
10. (many / much / a lot of) bottles
11. (many / much / a lot of) snow
12. (many / much / a lot of) toys

C. Look and write <many/much + noun>.

1.

(rice)

She doesn't have ___much rice___.

2.

(milk)

Does Karen drink _____?

3.

(book)

Sunny reads _____.

4.

(money)

I don't have _____.

Grammar in Writing

A. Put the words in the right order.

1. has / a lot of / Tom / problems

   ➡️ *Tom has a lot of problems* .

2. they / many / tigers / see

   ➡️ _____ .

3. I / much / don't have / money

   ➡️ _____ .

4. visited / a lot of / cities / we / in Korea

   ➡️ _____ .

5. Does / she / much / information / need / ?

   ➡️ _____ ?

B. Look and write.

1. 
   There are many(a lot of) eggs _____ but

   there aren't any apples .

   egg(O) / apple(X)

2. 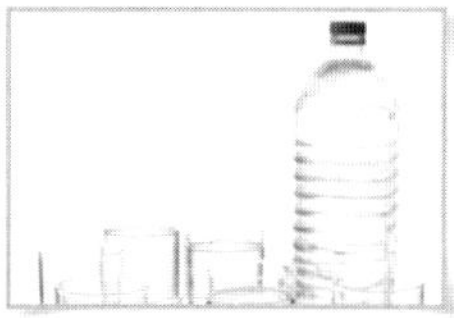
   _____ but

   _____ .

   water(O) / milk(X)

3. 
   _____ but

   _____ .

   bread(O) / orange(X)

Chapter 2

The Simple Present and Present Continuous

Be-verb

Grammar focus

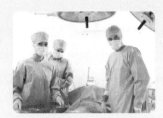

They are doctors.
They aren't nurses.
Are they doctors?
Yes, they are.

1. be동사가 뭐예요?

be동사에는 am, is, are 이렇게 세 가지가 있어요. 모양은 각기 다르지만 모두 앞의 주어와 뒤에 오는 단어를 연결해 주면서 '~이다, ~가 있다'의 뜻을 나타내요.

2. 부정문과 의문문은 어떻게 만드나요?

'~가 아니다, ~가 없다'라고 말하고 싶을 때는 be동사 바로 뒤에 not을 붙이면 돼요. 의문문은 be동사를 문장 맨 앞으로 보내고 물음표(?)를 붙여요. '~이니?, ~가 있니?'라는 뜻을 나타낸답니다.

Affirmative(긍정문)	Negative(부정문)	Question(의문문)
Kathy is happy. She is in the classroom.	Kevin isn't at the park. They aren't angry.	Is she a nurse? Are they alligators?

3. Contraction(축약형)

I'm	We're	You're	He's	She's	It's	They're
I'm not	We're not We aren't	You're not You aren't	He's not He isn't	She's not She isn't	It's not It isn't	They're not They aren't

Usage

Is he a taxi driver?
No, he **isn't**. He **is** a bus driver.

They **aren't** teachers.
They **are** bakers.

Go for it!

A. Read and circle the correct word.

1. You (am / (are) / is) very sad.
2. The sea (am / are / is) very deep.
3. We (am / are / is) in the first grade.
4. Some books (am / are / is) on the desk.
5. I (am / are / is) from Korea.
6. She (am / are / is) a doctor.
7. The children (am / are / is) happy.
8. I (am / are / is) a painter.
9. This (am / are / is) a big airplane.
10. These (am / are / is) books.
11. The men (am / are / is) strong.
12. We (am / are / is) police officers.

B. Look and fill in the blanks.

1.

They ___*aren't*___ teachers.
They ___*are*___ students.

2.

Sunny _____ a basketball player.
She _____ a tennis player.

3.

It _____ an MP3 player.
It _____ a cell phone.

4.

They _____ watermelons.
They _____ oranges.

C. Read and write *Am, Is* or *Are.*

1. __Are__ the women sad?   2. _____ he a dentist?

3. _____ she a singer?   4. _____ he an actor?

5. _____ they beautiful?   6. _____ we pilots?

7. _____ they puppies?   8. _____ I a bus driver?

9. _____ he your brother? 10. _____ Kevin and Nancy at the park?

D. Complete the question and check the correct answers.

1.
   ___Are___ ___they___ at home?
   ☐ Yes, they are. ☑ No, they aren't.

2.
   _____ _____ a cheetah?
   ☐ Yes, it is. ☐ No, they are.

3.
   _____ _____ at the bus stop?
   ☐ No, she is. ☐ No, she isn't.

Grammar in Writing

A. Look and fill in the blanks.

Name: Lisa
Age: 24
Job: student
Nationality: Switzerland
Marriage: single

Name: Peter
Age: 21
Job: office worker
Nationality: Italy
Marriage: single

1. _____Is she_____ a teacher? ➡ No, she isn't.

2. Is she young? ➡ Yes, _____.

3. _____ Italian? ➡ No, she isn't.

4. _____ 24 years old? ➡ Yes, she is.

5. Is she a student? ➡ Yes, _____.

6. _____ English? ➡ No, he isn't.

7. Is he a doctor? ➡ No, _____.

8. _____ single? ➡ Yes, he is.

9. Are they students? ➡ No, _____.

10. Are they young? ➡ Yes, _____.

11. _____ single? ➡ Yes, they are.

12. Are they American? ➡ No, _____.

Grammar focus

The girl **studies** English.
She **doesn't study** Japanese.
She **has** long hair.

1. 현재시제가 뭐예요?

우리가 표현하는 모든 동작을 나타내는 동사에는 시제가 있어요. 현재시제는 현재의 사실이나 반복되는 습관, 동작을 나타내요.

2. 왜 run에 -s를 붙여서 runs를 만드나요?

주어가 3인칭 단수(He, She, It, Tom, Mary …)일 경우에 동사 뒤에 보통 -s를 붙여 3인칭 단수형 동사라는 것을 표시해 줍니다.

❶ 대부분의 동사 뒤에 -s를 붙이면 돼요.

walk ➡ walk**s**   like ➡ like**s**   swim ➡ swim**s**

❷ -s, -ch, -sh, -x로 끝나는 동사는 -es를 붙여요.

wash ➡ wash**es**   teach ➡ teach**es**   fix ➡ fix**es**   kiss ➡ kiss**es**

❸ 〈자음+y〉로 끝나는 동사는 -y를 없애고 -ies를 붙여요.

study ➡ stud**ies**   cry ➡ cr**ies**   try ➡ tr**ies**   fly ➡ fl**ies**

3. 불규칙 동사가 뭐예요?

3인칭 단수가 주어인 경우, 대부분의 동사에는 규칙적으로 -s 또는 -es를 붙이는데, 불규칙 동사는 특별한 규칙이 없이 변해서 불규칙이라고 하는 거예요.

have ➡ has   go ➡ goes   do ➡ does

4. 부정문은 어떻게 만들어요?

'~않는다, ~아니다'의 의미인 부정문은 주어가 3인칭일 때는 〈doesn't+동사원형〉, 그 외엔 〈don't+동사원형〉으로 표현합니다.

Go for it!

A. Write the plural forms of the verbs.

1. watch ➡ *watches*
2. catch ➡ _____
3. cry ➡ _____
4. wash ➡ _____
5. fix ➡ _____
6. fly ➡ _____
7. brush ➡ _____
8. kiss ➡ _____
9. take ➡ _____
10. do ➡ _____
11. have ➡ _____
12. go ➡ _____
13. study ➡ _____
14. play ➡ _____

B. Look and circle the correct word.

1. We (doesn't / (don't)) do our homework.

2. He (doesn't / don't) have any money.

3. My sisters (doesn't / don't) play the piano.

4. You (doesn't / don't) read a book.

5. She (doesn't / don't) eat apples.

6. Lisa (doesn't / don't) study English.

7. My dad (doesn't / don't) do exercises.

8. Sunny (doesn't / don't) go to the church.

C. Look and fill in the blanks.

1.

coffee(X) ← drink → water(O)

Kathy _____*doesn't drink*_____ coffee.
She _____*drinks*_____ a lot of water.

2.

meat(X) ← like → vegetables(O)

The rabbit _____ meat.
It _____ vegetables.

3.

TV(X) ← watch → movie(O)

They _____ TV.
They _____ movies.

D. Look and circle the correct word.

1. (The girls / (The girl)) eats pizza.

2. (They / She) works at a bank.

3. (He / I) doesn't have much homework.

4. (We / Tom) have a puppy.

5. (Your sister / You) doesn't walk to school.

Grammar in Writing

A. Read and write.

1. *I wash my face.*
   I don't brush my teeth.

   Bob _washes his face_.
   Bob _doesn't brush his teeth_.

2. *I play the violin.*
   I don't play the piano.

   Lucy _____.
   Lucy _____.

3. *I do the dishes.*
   I don't do exercises.

   My mom _____.
   My mom _____.

4. *I listen to music.*
   I don't watch TV.

   Tiffany _____.
   Tiffany _____.

5. *I study English.*
   I don't study Chinese.

   Brian _____.
   Brian _____.

6. *I have a puppy.*
   I don't have a cat.

   Jane _____.
   Jane _____.

Yes/No Questions I

Grammar focus

Q: **Does** she walk to school?
A: **No**, she **doesn't**.

Q: **Does** she take a school bus?
A: **Yes**, she **does**.

1. 의문문은 어떻게 만들어요?

문장 맨 앞에 Do를 쓰고 문장 끝에 물음표(?)를 붙이면 돼요. 주어가 3인칭 단수인 경우에는 Does를 써요. 우리말로 '~하니, ~이니?'라는 의미입니다.

2. 대답은 어떻게 하나요?

be동사와 마찬가지로 Yes나 No로 대답하는 거예요. 긍정일 때는 〈Yes, 주어+do(does)〉, 부정일 때는 〈No, 주어+don't(doesn't)〉로 짧게 하면 돼요.

Yes / No Question & Answer	
1, 2인칭 단·복수/3인칭 복수	3인칭 단수
Q: Do you like music?	Q: Does he ride a bicycle?
A: Yes, I do. / No, I don't.	A: Yes, she does. / No, she doesn't.

Usage

Q: **Does** she brush her teeth?
A: **Yes**, she **does**.

Q: **Does** he fly a kite?
A: **Yes**, he **does**.

Q: **Do** they read books?
A: **No**, they **don't**.

Go for it!

A. Write and match.

1.

2.

3.

4.

Q: _____ he read a magazine?
A: No, he doesn't.

Q: _____ she play soccer?
A: No, she doesn't.

Q: _Does_ she jog?
A: Yes, she does.

Q: _____ they have hats?
A: Yes, they do.

B. Write the answers.

1. Do you speak English?   Yes, _____ _I do_ _____.

2. Does Bob listen to music?   No, _____.

3. Do the children walk to school? Yes, _____.

4. Does she like horror moives?   No, _____.

C. Read and circle the correct word.

1. (Do / (Does)) Karen (plays / (play)) the violin?

2. (Do / Does) he (reads / read) a book?

3. (Do / Does) the baby (sleep / sleeps) for 10 hours?

4. (Do / Does) it (drinks / drink) much water?

5. (Do / Does) they (put / puts) on the red shirts?

D. Write questions. Then, write negative sentences.

1. Sunny likes green tea.
   → *Does Sunny like green tea* ?
   → *Sunny doesn't like green tea* .

2. He plays basketball on Saturdays.
   → _____ ?
   → _____ .

3. Rachel lives in Seoul, Korea.
   → _____ ?
   → _____ .

4. They work at a big hospital.
   → _____ ?
   → _____ .

Grammar in Writing

A. Write the questions and answers.

1. she / like / pizza

    ➥ _Does she like pizza_____ ? _Yes, she does_ . _No, she doesn't_ .

2. they / eat / lunch

    ➥ _____ ? _____ . _____ .

3. rabbits / have / long ears

    ➥ _____ ? _____ . _____ .

4. he / wash / his feet

    ➥ _____ ? _____ . _____ .

B. Look at the chart. Make questions and answers.

	I	He	She	They
live in Korea	O	X	O	O
play the drum	X	O	X	X
like shopping	O	X	O	X
speak Japenese very well	X	O	X	O

1. I / live in Korea

    ➥ _Do you live in Korea_____ ? _Yes, I do_ .

2. she / play the drum

    ➥ _____ ? _____ .

3. she / like shopping

    ➥ _____ ? _____ .

4. he / speak Japanese very well

    ➥ _____ ? _____ .

5. they / live in Korea

    ➥ _____ ? _____ .

Present Continuous I

Grammar focus

Q: **Is** she play**ing** the drum?
A: **No**, she **isn't**. She **is playing** the violin.

1. 현재 진행형이 뭐예요?

진행형은 여러분들이 지금 보고 있는 순간에 진행 중인 동작이나 행동을 표현하는 동사의 시제 중에 하나예요. 형태는 언제나 〈be동사(am/is/are)+Ⓥ-ing〉예요. '~하고 있다, ~ 하고 있는 중이다'라는 뜻으로, 부정문은 be동사 뒤에 not을 붙이면 되고, 의문문은 be동사를 문장 앞으로 보내고 물음표(?)를 붙이면 돼요.

Affirmative(긍정문)	Negative(부정문)	Question(의문문)
I am going to school now.	He isn't walking.	Is she reading a book?
She is eating.	They aren't watching TV.	Are the boys swimming?

2. 동사의 진행형은 어떻게 만드나요?

❶ 대부분의 동사원형에 -ing를 붙여요.

go ➡ going   eat ➡ eating   work ➡ working   see ➡ seeing
teach ➡ teaching   do ➡ doing   buy ➡ buying

❷ -e로 끝나는 동사는 -e를 지우고 -ing를 붙여요.

take ➡ taking   come ➡ coming   live ➡ living   make ➡ making

❸ 〈단모음+단자음〉으로 끝나는 동사는 마지막 자음철자를 한 번 더 쓰고 -ing를 붙여요.

sit ➡ sitting   swim ➡ swimming   run ➡ running

Usage

They **aren't** sing**ing**.
They **are** danc**ing**.

She **isn't** watch**ing** TV.
She **is** listen**ing** to music.

Are they runn**ing**?
No, they aren't.
They **are** walk**ing**.

Go for it!

A. Look and write.

	I			He / Tom / Kevin	
	Base verb	be + Ⓥ-ing		Base verb	be + Ⓥ-ing
1.	see	*am seeing*	2.	write	*is writing*
3.	swim	_____	4.	begin	_____
5.	work	_____	6.	sit	_____

	She / Susan / Lucy			They / You / We	
	Base verb	be + Ⓥ-ing		Base verb	be + Ⓥ-ing
7.	make	_____	8.	listen	_____
9.	come	_____	10.	have	_____
11.	run	_____	12.	do	_____
13.	stop	_____	14.	live	_____
15.	study	_____	16.	go	_____

B. Choose and write.

play	eat	wash	read

1.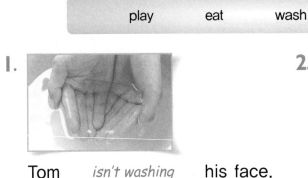

Tom _isn't washing_ his face.
He _is washing_ his hands.

2.

Nacny _____ a newspaper.
She _____ a magazine.

3.

Kelly _____ an orange.
She _____ an apple.

4.

Lucy _____ the piano.
She _____ the violin.

C. Look and make questions.

1.

(she / eat a hamburger)

Q: _Is she eating a hamburger_ ?

2.

(they / wash the car)

Q: _____ ?

3.

(they / dance)

Q: _____ ?

4.

(she / drive a car)

Q: _____ ?

Grammar in Writing

A. Make the negatives and questions.

1. is / Lucy / on the sofa / sleep
   - ⟹ *Lucy isn't sleeping on the sofa* _____ .
   - ⟹ *Is Lucy sleeping on the sofa* _____ ?

2. are / in the pool / swim / Lucy and Tom
   - ⟹ _____ .
   - ⟹ _____ ?

3. is / Tom / on the bench / sit
   - ⟹ _____ .
   - ⟹ _____ ?

B. Look at the pictures. Make questions and answers.

1.	2.	3.
(jog in the park)	(have a snowball fight)	(dance with his wife)

1. She / read a book
   - Q: *Is she reading a book* _____ ?
   - A: *No, she isn't. She's jogging in the park* _____ .

2. They / make a snowman
   - Q: _____ ?
   - A: _____ .

3. He / sing a song
   - Q: _____ ?
   - A: _____ .

Chapter 3
The Future Tense

Grammar focus

She has a test tomorrow.
She **will study** hard.

It **won't be** sunny tomorrow.

1. 미래시제는 어떻게 쓰나요?

❶ '~할 거야, ~일 거야'처럼 앞으로의 일을 말하거나 미래의 일을 예상할 때 쓰는 미래시제는 동사 앞에 will을 써서 미래를 표현해요. will 뒤에는 항상 동사원형을 쓰므로 will buys 또는 will are처럼 쓰지 않도록 유의해야 합니다.

❷ 지금 현재 순간적(즉흥적)으로 결정할 때에도 will을 사용해요.

2. 부정문은 어떻게 만드나요?

'~하지 않을 거야'라는 의미의 부정문을 만들고 싶을 때는 will 뒤에 not을 붙이면 돼요. will not을 써도 좋지만 축약해서 won't를 많이 써요.

Future Tense			
Affirmative(긍정문): will		Negative(부정문): will not(=won't)	
I / You / We / They He / She / It	will come tomorrow.	I / You / We / They He / She / It	will not come tomorrow.

Usage

It **will be** sunny tomorrow.
We **will play** tennis tomorrow.

My mom is angry at me.
I **won't listen** to music any more.

Go for it!

A. Circle the correct word.

1. She will (sings / (sing)) a song.

2. Mary will (draws / draw) a picture.

3. Ted will (does / do) his homework tomorrow.

4. It (rains / rain) a lot in summer in Korea.

5. They will (are / be) middle school students next year.

6. My dad will (stops / stop) smoking.

7. She (is / be) a singer.

8. We (eats / eat) breakfast everyday.

B. Write *will* or *won't*.

1.

They __won't__ watch TV.
They __will__ eat dinner.

2.

He _____ wear boots tomorrow.
He _____ wear sneakers tomorrow.

3.

She _____ go shopping.
She _____ stay at home.

4.

We _____ do our homework.
We _____ visit the zoo.

C. Change the sentences with *will* or *won't*.

1. I go to the movie theater.
   → I _____*will go*_____ to the movie theater.

2. She drinks some milk.
   → She _____ some milk.

3. Kelly doesn't open the window.
   → Kelly _____ the window.

4. Mom buys some bread.
   → Mom _____ some bread.

5. He visits my house soon.
   → He _____ my house soon.

6. My brother doesn't clean his room.
   → My brother _____ his room.

D. Look and fill in the blanks.

1.
   (read)

   Lucy _____*won't read*_____ a newspaper.
   Lucy _____*will read*_____ a book.

2.
   (play)

   Jane _____ basketball tomorrow.
   Jane _____ soccer tomorrow.

3.
   (be)

   It _____ sunny tomorrow.
   It _____ rainy tomorrow.

A. Look and write.

☐ listen to music
☒ clean her room
☐ go shopping
☒ join the dance club
☐ go to the park

Q: What will Lucy do tomorrow?

1. *Lucy will listen to music tomorrow* .

2. _____ .

3. _____ .

4. _____ .

5. _____ .

B. Look and write.

1.

(buy it)
I really like this dress.
I will buy it .

2.

(eat lunch)
They are very hungry.
_____ .

3.

(clean the house)
My house is dirty.
_____ .

4.

(take a taxi)
They are late for work.
_____ .

unit 2 — Will + S + Ⓥ ~?

Q: **Will** she do the laundry tomorrow?
A: **Yes**, she **will**.
No, she **won't**.

1. 미래시제가 쓰인 의문문은 어떻게 만드나요?

Will을 문장 맨 앞으로 보내고 물음표(?)를 써주면 돼요. 〈Will+주어+동사원형 ~?〉 형태가 됩니다.

2. 대답은 어떻게 하나요?

Yes나 No로 답하고, 긍정일 때 〈Yes, 주어+will.〉 부정일 때는 〈No, 주어+won't.〉로 합니다.

Questions	Answers	
Will you study tomorrow?	Yes, I will.	No, I won't.
Will she go shopping?	Yes, she will.	No, she won't.
Will he go fishing?	Yes, he will.	No, he won't.
Will they go to the zoo?	Yes, they will.	No, they won't.
Will it be windy tomorrow?	Yes, it will.	No, it won't.

Usage

Q: **Will** the boy **play** computer games?
A: **Yes**, he **will**.

Q: **Will** she **go** fishing tomorrow?
A: **No**, she **won't**.
She **will go** shopping tomorrow.

46

Go for it!

A. Match and write.

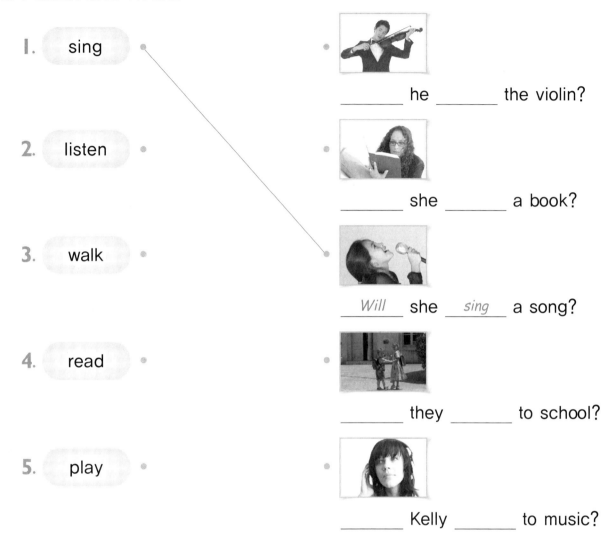

1. sing

_____ he _____ the violin?

2. listen

_____ she _____ a book?

3. walk

Will she _sing_ a song?

4. read

_____ they _____ to school?

5. play

_____ Kelly _____ to music?

B. Look and complete the answers.

1. Will Rachel buy the car? → Yes, _____she will_____.

2. Will they visit the zoo? → No, _____.

3. Will Kevin swim in the pool? → Yes, _____.

4. Will Sunny paint a picture? → No, _____.

5. Will we have dinner? → Yes, _____.

C. Change the sentences.

1. He will play tennis tomorrow.

    → _____*Will he play*_____ tennis tomorrow?

2. She will write an English letter.

    → _____ an English letter?

3. Rachel will buy a new hat.

    → _____ a new hat?

4. They will play soccer next week.

    → _____ soccer next week?

D. Look at the pictures and write answers.

1.

    Q: Will it rain tomorrow?

    A: *Yes, it will*_____ .

2.

    Q: Will Lucy clean the room?

    A: _____ .

3.

    Q: Will the boy play computer games?

    A: _____ .

4.

    Q: Will she watch a movie?

    A: _____ .

Grammar in Writing

A. Make questions.

What will Jennifer do tomorrow?
1. go to the park (O)   2. do her homework (X)
3. buy a game CD (O)   4. meet her friends (O)
5. do the dishes (X)   6. ride a bicycle (O)

1. *Will Jennifer go to the park tomorrow* ? ➡ Yes, she will.

2. _____ ? ➡ No, she won't.

3. _____ ? ➡ Yes, she will.

4. _____ ? ➡ Yes, she will.

5. _____ ? ➡ No, she won't.

6. _____ ? ➡ Yes, she will.

B. Look and write answers.

1.

(jog)

Q: Will she cook breakfast tomorrow morning?
A: *No, she won't* .
   She will jog tomorrow morning .

2.

(paint the house)

Q: Will they wash their car tomorrow?
A: _____ .
   _____ .

49

I'm (not) going to Ⓥ ~

Grammar focus

He **is going to** go to Hong Kong next Friday.

Look at those black clouds!
It **is going to** rain soon.

1. be going to가 뭐예요?

〈be going to+동사원형〉은 가까운 미래에 생길 일이나 이미 마음 속에 결정이 내려진 일을 말할 때 써요. '~할 것이다, ~할 예정이다'의 뜻으로 이미 예정된 계획은 will을 쓰지 않고 be going to로 표현해요.

Affirmative(긍정): Subject+be+going to Ⓥ		
I	am	
You/We/They	are	going to eat.
He/She/It	is	

2. 부정문은 어떻게 만드나요?

부정문을 만들 때는 be동사 뒤에 not을 붙이면 돼요. '~하지 않을 거야'라는 뜻이에요.

Negative(부정): Subject+be not+going to Ⓥ		
I	am	
You/We/They	are	not going to eat.
He/She/It	is	

Usage

They **are not going to** study.
They **are going to** have breakfast.

She **is not going to** drink juice.
She **is going to** eat the apple.

Go for it!

A. Circle the correct word.

1. I (are / is / (am)) not going to play soccer.

2. She (are / is / am) going to learn English.

3. He (are / is / am) going to go skiing.

4. Nancy (are / is / am) going to go shopping.

5. My dad (are / is / am) going to go fishing.

6. We (are / is / am) going to clean the classroom.

7. They (are / is / am) going to watch TV.

B. Change the sentences to the negative.

1. She is going to read a book.
   ➡ *She is not going to read a book* .

2. He is going to tell the truth.
   ➡ _____ .

3. Kevin and Jane are going to buy CDs.
   ➡ _____ .

4. I am going to walk to school.
   ➡ _____ .

5. They are going to sleep.
   ➡ _____ .

C. Complete the sentences using *be going to*.

1. Kelly has a basketball.
   She _____*is going to play*_____ basketball. (play)

2. Tom has a book.
   He _____ the book. (read)

3. They are at home.
   They _____ a movie. (watch)

4. Sunny and Tiffany have a digital camera.
   They _____ a picture. (take)

D. Correct the underline words and rewrite.

1. My mom <u>are</u> going to make some cookies.
   → *My mom is going to make some cookies* .

2. We are going to <u>visits</u> the zoo tomorrow.
   → _____ .

3. She <u>not is</u> going to wash the dishes.
   → _____ .

4. He is going to <u>bought</u> a new bicycle.
   → _____ .

Grammar in Writing

A. Choose and write.

| drink a cup of coffee | rain soon |
| eat the hamburger | buy some fruit |

1.

She is very hungry.

She is going to eat the hamburger .

2.

Look at those black clouds.

_____ .

3.

Lisa is in the market.

_____ .

4.

Bob is in a cafe.

_____ .

B. Look at the chart and make sentences.

My Winter Vacation Plan			
1. learn to swim	O	2. visit my aunt in Rome	X
3. play tennis	X	4. study Japanese	O

1. *I am going to learn to swim* .

2. _____ .

3. _____ .

4. _____ .

unit 4 Be + S + going to Ⓥ ~ ?

Grammar focus

Q: **Is** she **going to** ride a bicycle?
A: No, she isn't. She is going to ride a horse.

1. 의문문은 어떻게 만드나요?

Be동사가 있는 의문문처럼 be동사를 문장 맨 앞으로 보내고 물음표(?)를 붙여서 의문문을 만들어요.
우리말로 '~할거니?, ~할 예정이니?'의 뜻이에요.

2. 답은 어떻게 하나요?

긍정일 때 〈Yes, 주어+be.〉, 부정일 때는 〈No, 주어+be not.〉으로 대답해요.

Questions (Be+Subject+going to Ⓥ ~?)		
Am I going to ~ ?	➡	Yes, you are. / No, you aren't.
Are you going to ~ ?	➡	Yes, I am. / No, I am not.
Are we going to ~ ?	➡	Yes, we are. / No, we aren't.
Are they going to ~ ?	➡	Yes, they are. / No, they aren't.
Is she going to ~ ?	➡	Yes, she is. / No, she isn't.
Is he going to ~ ?	➡	Yes, he is. / No, he isn't.
Is it going to ~ ?	➡	Yes, it is. / No, it isn't.

Usage

Q: **Is** the girl **going to** study English?
A: Yes, she is.

Q: **Are** they **going to** go to the park?
A: No, they aren't.
   They are going to go to the library.

Go for it!

A. Match and write.

1. (he)
2. (she)
3. (they)
4. (you)

_____
have a party?

Is he going to
_____
listen to music?

_____
travel by train?

_____
go skiing?

B. Complete the answers.

1. A: Are the children going to take the school bus?
   B: Yes, _____ *they are* _____ .

2. A: Is Susan going to meet him?
   B: No, _____ .

3. A: Is Brian going to buy the iPhone?
   B: Yes, _____ .

4. A: Are the girls going to fly kites?
   B: No, _____ .

C. Read and make questions.

1. A: *Is Scott going to buy a gift* _____?
   B: Yes, Scott is going to buy a gift.

2. A: _____?
   B: Yes, I'm going to learn Chinese.

3. A: _____?
   B: Yes, they are going to go to Jeju Island.

4. A: _____?
   B: Yes, she is going to fly a kite.

5. A: _____?
   B: Yes, he is going to walk to school.

D. Read and answer the questions.

1.
   Q: Is the girl going to drink tea?
   A: ___*No*___, _____*she isn't*_____.

2.
   Q: Is the woman going to play tennis?
   A: _____, _____.

3.
   Q: Is your mom going to take a shower?
   A: _____, _____.

Grammar in Writing

A. Look at the pictures and answer the questions.

1.

   (sleep)

   Q: Are they going to go to the park?
   A: *No, they aren't. They are going to sleep*   .

2.

   (buy new shoes)

   Q: Is she going to visit your house?
   A: _____ .

3.

   (play computer games)

   Q: Is the boy going to watch a movie?
   A: _____ .

B. Look at David's diary for next week. Answer the questions.

David's Dirary			
• Monday	play volleyball	• Thursday	learn to swim
• Tuesday	play tennis	• Friday	go to a museum
• Wednesday	study English	• Saturday	go skiing

1. Q: Is David going to play soccer next Monday?
   A: *No, he isn't. He's going to play volleyball*   .

2. Q: Is David going to play tennis next Tuesday?
   A: _____ .

3. Q: Is David going to study Japanese next Wednesday?
   A: _____ .

4. Q: Is David going to go to a museum next Saturday?
   A: _____ .

Chapter 4
The Past Tense

unit 1 *Positives*

Grammar focus

Lisa **washed** her hair yesterday.

Lisa **is talking** on the phone now.

1. 과거시제는 어떻게 만드나요?

과거시제는 다음과 같이 일정한 규칙에 의해서 만들어요.

❶ 대부분의 동사는 -ed를 붙여서 과거동사를 만들어요.

❷ -e로 끝나는 동사는 그냥 -d만 붙이면 돼요.

❸ 동사 끝에 〈자음+y〉로 끝나면 y를 i로 고치고 -ed를 붙여요.

The Simple Past – Regular Verbs			
verb+-ed		verb+-d	drop y+-ied
help ➡ helped	invent ➡ invented	dance ➡ danced	study ➡ studied
work ➡ worked	talk ➡ talked	live ➡ lived	try ➡ tried
wash ➡ washed	paint ➡ painted	like ➡ liked	cry ➡ cried
rain ➡ rained	visit ➡ visited	love ➡ loved	carry ➡ carried
clean ➡ cleaned	listen ➡ listened	notice ➡ noticed	

2. 불규칙 과거동사가는 뭔가요?

규칙적으로 동사에 '-(e)d'를 붙여 과거동사를 만들지 않고 불규칙하게 변하는 동사를 말해요.

The Simple Past – Irregular Verbs					
go ➡ went	have ➡ had	come ➡ came
begin ➡ began	hear ➡ heard	find ➡ found
give ➡ gave	leave ➡ left	see ➡ saw
eat ➡ ate	make ➡ made	sing ➡ sang
write ➡ wrote	buy ➡ bought	read ➡ read
meet ➡ met	drive ➡ drove	sit ➡ sat
get ➡ got	speak ➡ spoke	ride ➡ rode

Go for it!

A. Write the verbs into the past tense.

1. go → _went_

2. play → _____

3. eat → _____

4. help → _____

5. meet → _____

6. walk → _____

7. leave → _____

8. study → _____

9. buy → _____

10. listen → _____

11. speak → _____

12. try → _____

13. drive → _____

14. love → _____

15. begin → _____

16. visit → _____

17. write → _____

18. paint → _____

19. have → _____

20. live → _____

21. make → _____

22. cry → _____

23. find → _____

24. rain → _____

B. Complete the sentences with the past tense.

1.
(listen to music)

She ___*listened to music*___ .

2.
(rain yesterday)

It _____ .

3.
(buy a new bag)

The girl _____ .

4.
(watch a movie)

We _____ .

C. Write the correct tense of the verb.

1.
(listen)

He ___*listens*___ to music every day.

He ___*listened*___ to music yesterday.

2.
(walk)

They _____ to school every day.

They _____ to school yesterday.

3.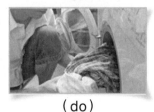
(go)

The boy _____ skateboarding every day.

The boy _____ skateboarding last night.

4.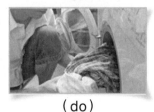
(do)

He usually _____ the laundry.

He _____ the laundry yesterday.

Grammar in Writing

A. Make sentences with the past tense.

1.

She / a car / drive

1. _She drove a car_ .

2. _____ .

3. _____ .

4. _____ .

2.

sit / Susan / on the bench

3.

we / Korea / last year / visit

4.

buy / he / a gift

B. Look at the pictures and write the answers.

1.

(a letter)

Q: What did she write yesterday?

A: _She wrote a letter_ .

2.

(wash the dishes)

Q: What did they do yesterday?

A: _____ .

3.

(take pictures)

Q: What did he do yesterday?

A: _____ .

4.

(noodles)

Q: What did Mary eat yesterday?

A: _____ .

unit 2 Negatives

Grammar focus

She **studied** English yesterday.
She **didn't study** Japanese.

We **didn't visit** Seoul last year.
We **visited** Paris.

1. 과거시제가 쓰인 부정문은 어떻게 만드나요?

주어가 3인칭 단수이든, 복수이든 관계없이 동사 앞에 did not(=didn't)를 쓰고, 동사는 원형 그대로 써주면 돼요.

주어 + did not + 동사원형 ~			
I/We/You He/She/It/They	did not(=didn't)	drink	coffee.

Usage

I saw a tiger yesterday.
I **didn't see** an elephant.

We went on a picnic yesterday.
We **didn't go** fishing.

Go for it!

A. Circle the correct word.

1. She didn't (met / (meet)) Kevin.

2. Peter didn't (go / went) to the park yesterday.

3. Wilson (do / did) his homework yesterday.

4. They (ate / eat) pizza yesterday.

5. Scott didn't (took / take) the bus to school.

6. We didn't (plays / play) basketball yesterday.

B. Look and complete the sentences.

1.

   play tennis (X)
   do the dishes (O)

   She _____*didn't play*_____ tennis yesterday.
   She _____*did*_____ the dishes.

2.
   listen to music (X)
   finish her homework (O)

   The girl _____ to music yesterday.
   She _____ her homework.

3.
   walk to school (X)
   take the school bus (O)

   Tiffany _____ to school yesterday.
   She _____ the school bus.

C. Write *don't, doesn't* or *didn't*.

1. We ____*didn't*____ go to the museum last weekend.

2. Lisa is afraid of mice. She _____ like them.

3. He _____ get up early every morning.

4. I _____ help my mom yesterday.

5. The children _____ brush their teeth every morning.

D. Make the sentences positive(P) and negative(N) in the simple past.

1. She has a puppy.
   P: *She had a puppy*_____. N: *She didn't have a puppy*_____.

2. I brush my teeth.
   P: _____. N: _____.

3. He takes a tennis lesson.
   P: _____. N: _____.

4. Brown goes camping.
   P: _____. N: _____.

5. They watch TV.
   P: _____. N: _____.

Grammar in Writing

A. Look at the table and make sentences.

Things Done (yesterday)	Kevin	Lisa
1. listen to music	O	X
2. go to the library	X	O
3. write an e-mail	X	O
4. walk for 20 minutes	O	X

1. Kevin _____listened to music yesterday_____.
   Lisa _____didn't listen to music yesterday_____.

2. Kevin _____.
   Lisa _____.

3. Kevin _____.
   Lisa _____.

4. Kevin _____.
   Lisa _____.

B. Look at the picture and make sentences with the simple past.

1. the child / wear / a hat
   ⇒ _____The child didn't wear a hat_____.

2. they / watch / television
   ⇒ _____.

3. they / eat / fast food
   ⇒ _____.

4. she / read / a book / to her daughter
   ⇒ _____.

Unit 3 Yes/No Questions Ⅱ

Grammar focus

A: **Did** they **go** to the zoo?
B: **No**, they **didn't**.
A: **Did** they **go** fishing?
B: **Yes**, they **did**.

1. **과거시제로 의문문은 어떻게 만들어요?**

   문장 맨 앞에 Did를 쓰고 문장 끝에 물음표(?)를 붙이면 돼요. '~했니, ~했었니?'라는 뜻으로 Did가
   과거임을 알리는 역할을 하기 때문에 동사는 과거를 만들지 않고 동사원형 그대로 써야 해요.

2. **대답은 어떻게 하나요?**

   be동사와 마찬가지로 일반 동사의 의문문도 Yes나 No로 대답하는 거예요. 긍정일 때는 〈Yes, 주어+
   did.〉, 부정일 때는 〈No, 주어+didn't.〉로 짧게 대답해요.

Q	Did	I / you / we / he / she / it / they ~	ⓥ ~ ?
A	Yes, S did. / No, S didn't.		

Usage

Q: **Did** you **play** volleyball?
A: **Yes**, I **did**.

Q: **Did** she **buy** a new car?
A: **Yes**, she **did**.

Q: **Did** he **cook** lunch at home?
A: **No**, he **didn't**.

Q: **Did** they **play** computer games?
A: **No**, they **didn't**.

Go for it!

A. Circle the correct word.

1. Did you (get / got / gets) up at 6?

2. Did Bob (play / plays / played) soccer?

3. She didn't (have / has / had) a good time.

4. He didn't (gave / gives / give) me a book.

5. Did they (dances / danced / dance) at the party?

6. The concert didn't (began / begins / begin) at 9.

7. Did she (wear / wears / wore) a nice dress?

B. Look and match.

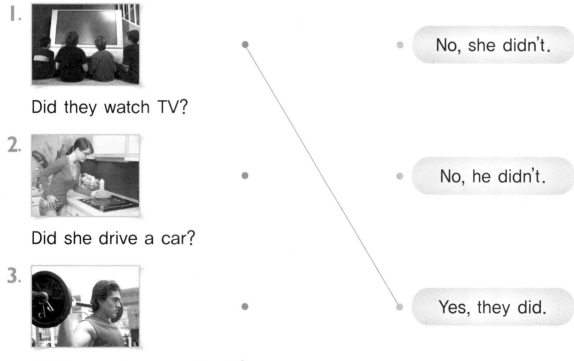

1. Did they watch TV?

2. Did she drive a car?

3. Did he read a scary book?

No, she didn't.

No, he didn't.

Yes, they did.

C. Make questions and answer them.

1. ___Did___ ___you___ eat the hamburger?   → No, I ___didn't___ .

2. _____ _____ sleep late?   → Yes, she _____ .

3. _____ _____ visit Buckingham Palace?   → No, I _____ .

4. _____ _____ go camping last year?   → Yes, they _____ .

5. _____ _____ have lunch at home?   → No, he _____ .

6. _____ _____ snow yesterday?   → Yes, it _____ .

D. Look at the pictures and write answers.

1.

Q: Did she ride a horse?
A: _Yes, she did._____ .

2.

Q: Did you listen to music?
A: _____ .

3.

Q: Did it snow yesterday?
A: _____ .

4.

Q: Did they go to a movie theater?
A: _____ .

Grammar in Writing

A. Look and answer the questions.

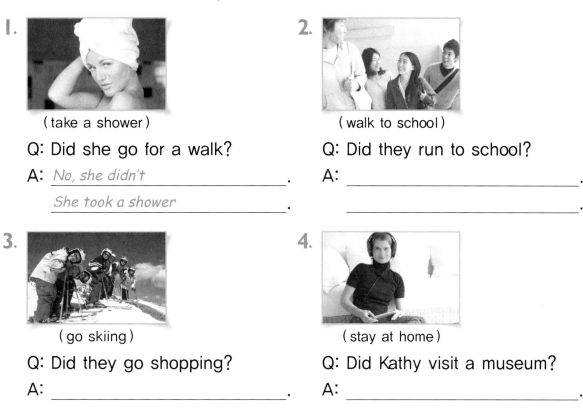

1.

(take a shower)

Q: Did she go for a walk?

A: *No, she didn't* .

She took a shower .

2.

(walk to school)

Q: Did they run to school?

A: _____ .

_____ .

3.

(go skiing)

Q: Did they go shopping?

A: _____ .

_____ .

4.

(stay at home)

Q: Did Kathy visit a museum?

A: _____ .

_____ .

B. Look at the pictures and make questions and answers.

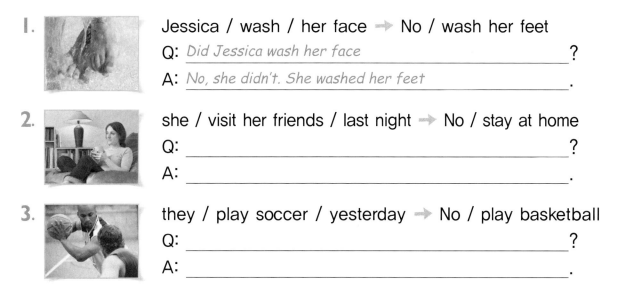

1.

Jessica / wash / her face ➡ No / wash her feet

Q: *Did Jessica wash her face* ?

A: *No, she didn't. She washed her feet* .

2.

she / visit her friends / last night ➡ No / stay at home

Q: _____ ?

A: _____ .

3.

they / play soccer / yesterday ➡ No / play basketball

Q: _____ ?

A: _____ .

unit 4 · *What did ~ ?* & *Past Continuous* I

Grammar focus

Q: **What** did she buy?
A: She bought the cell phone.

They **were sleeping** at 10:00 yesterday.

1. what으로 시작되는 과거시제 의문문은 어떻게 만드나요?

〈What+did+주어+동사원형 ~ ?〉의 어순으로 만들어요. Yes나 No로 대답할 수 없어요.

What	did	Subject(주어)	Ⓥ (동사원형) ~ ?
What	did	I / we / you she / he / it they	cook?

2. 과거진행형이 뭔가요?

과거진행형은 과거에 어떤 동작이 진행, 계속되고 있었음을 나타내요. 〈be+Ⓥ-ing〉의 형태로 만들어 주고 과거의 진행 중인 동작을 나타내야 하므로 be동사는 주어가 단수이면 was, 주어가 복수이면 were을 써주면 돼.

Subject(주어)	Be Verb(be동사)	Ⓥ-ing
I / She / He / it	was	sleeping.
We / You / They	were	

Usage

Q: **What** did she have?
A: She had a ball.

She **was playing** the violin.

They **were running** to school.

Go for it!

A. Match and fill in the blanks.

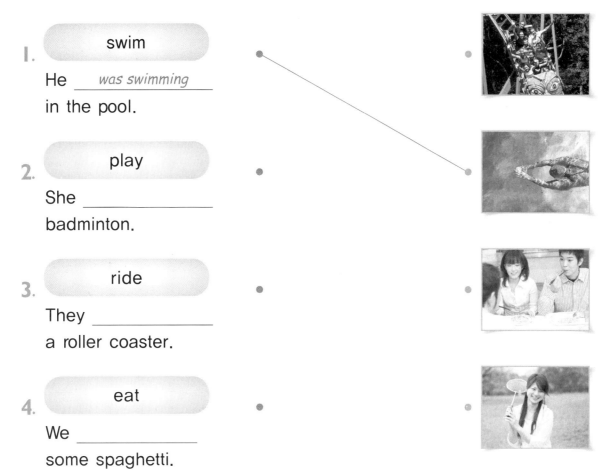

1. swim

He ___was swimming___ in the pool.

2. play

She _____ badminton.

3. ride

They _____ a roller coaster.

4. eat

We _____ some spaghetti.

B. Read and complete the dialog.

1. Q: What did Sunny ___study___? (study)
   A: ___She studied___ English.

2. Q: What did Bob _____? (eat)
   A: _____ some sandwiches.

C. Change the verbs in the past continuous.

1. see   → I _____ *was seeing* _____

2. write   → He _____

3. swim   → You _____

4. begin   → They _____

5. make   → She _____

6. listen   → We _____

7. come   → He _____

8. have   → Bob _____

9. run   → Susan _____

10. do   → You _____

D. Look and make questions.

1. what / you / bought   → *What did you buy* _____?

2. what / he / ate   → _____?

3. what / she / made / yesterday → _____?

4. what / they / did / last night → _____?

Grammar in Writing

A. Look at the picures. Answer the questions.

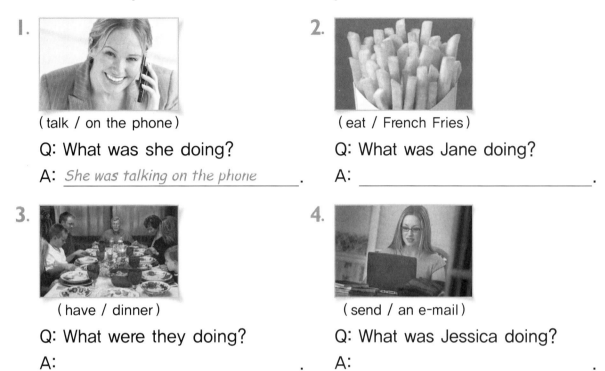

1.

(talk / on the phone)

Q: What was she doing?

A: *She was talking on the phone* .

2.

(eat / French Fries)

Q: What was Jane doing?

A: _____ .

3.

(have / dinner)

Q: What were they doing?

A: _____ .

4.

(send / an e-mail)

Q: What was Jessica doing?

A: _____ .

B. Look at the table and make questions and answers.

	drink some coffee	make cookies	eat cheeseburgers
Jessica	O	X	O
Bob and Jane	X	O	O

1. A: Did Jessica drink orange juice?

   B: No, she didn't.

   A: *What did she drink* ?

   B: *She drank some coffee* .

2. A: Did Bob and Jane make cakes?

   B: No, they didn't.

   A: _____ ?

   B: _____ .

3. A: Did Jessica eat French Fries?

   B: No, she didn't.

   A: _____ ?

   B: _____ .

4. A: Did Bob and Jane eat pizza?

   B: No, they didn't.

   A: _____ ?

   B: _____ .

75

Chapter 5
Adverbs & Adjectives

unit 1 *Adverbs*

My mom drives **carefully**.
She is a good driver.

1. 부사가 뭐예요?

형용사가 명사를 구체적으로 설명해 주는 역할이라면 부사는 동사를 더욱 구체적으로 설명해 주는 역할을 해요. 주로 동사 뒤나, 문장 맨 뒤에 쓰고 우리말로 '~하게'로 해석되는 경우가 많아요.

2. 부사는 어떻게 만드나요?

부사는 대개 형용사에 -ly를 붙여 만들어요. 형용사와 부사의 모양이 같은 것들도 있어요.

adjective+-ly=adverb				different changes	no change
slow	➡ slowly	kind	➡ kindly		
loud	➡ loudly	easy	➡ easily		fast ➡ fast
real	➡ really	happy	➡ happily		early ➡ early
careful	➡ carefully	bad	➡ badly	good ➡ well	late ➡ late
quick	➡ quickly	beautiful	➡ beautifully		hard ➡ hard
large	➡ largely	wise	➡ wisely		
quiet	➡ quietly	sad	➡ sadly		

Usage

The elephant walks **slowly**.

Tom is a good swimmer.
He swims **well**.

Go for it!

slowly	kind	fast	hard
easily	careful	quick	loudly
early	late	happily	beautiful
badly	happy	largely	really

A. Choose adjectives and write.

1. _____kind_____　　2. _____　　3. _____

4. _____　　5. _____

B. Choose adverbs and write.

6. ____slowly____　　7. _____　　8. _____

9. _____　　10. _____　　11. _____

12. _____

C. Choose <adjective=adverb> and write.

13. _____fast_____　　14. _____　　15. _____

16. _____

D. Write the adverb forms.

1. real   →   *really*

2. slow   →   _____

3. happy   →   _____

4. quick   →   _____

5. easy   →   _____

6. loud   →   _____

7. good   →   _____

8. fast   →   _____

9. late   →   _____

10. kind   →   _____

11. careful   →   _____

12. wise   →   _____

E. Match and write.

1. **beautiful**

They dance

_____*beautifully*_____.

2. **happy**

They are smiling

_____.

3. **hard**

They are studying

_____.

4. **quick**

The cheetah runs

_____.

Grammar in Writing

A. Find the mistakes in the sentences and rewrite them correctly.

1. The bird flies fastly. ➡ *The bird flies fast* .

2. The snail moves slow. ➡ _____ .

3. He plays the piano good. ➡ _____ .

4. The girl is playing the drum loud. ➡ _____ .

5. I real like apples. ➡ _____ .

6. The girl is dancing beautiful. ➡ _____ .

7. They walk quiet in the hallway. ➡ _____ .

B. Look at the pictures. Answer the questions.

1.

(late)

Q: Did she get up early?

A: *No, she didn't* .

She got up late .

2.

(happy)

Q: Did she dance sadly?

A: _____ .

_____ .

3.

(loud)

Q: Did she shout quietly?

A: _____ .

_____ .

4.

(fast)

Q: Does it run slowly?

A: _____ .

_____ .

Frequency Adverbs

Grammar focus

Kathy **always** walks to school.
She is **often** late for school.
She **seldom** does homework.

1. 빈도 부사가 뭐예요?

빈도부사란 어떤 일이 발생하는 횟수(빈도)를 나타내 주는 부사를 말해요.

2. 빈도부사의 위치는 어떻게 되나요?

일반 동사 앞에 쓰고, be동사 뒤에 써야 해요.

always	usually	often	sometimes	seldom/hardly	never
100%	about 90%	about 70%	about 50%	about 10%	0%
(항상)	(대개, 보통)	(자주, 종종)	(때때로)	(거의 ~ 않다)	(결코 ~않다)

Usage

The students are **always** happy.
└─ (be동사 뒤)

Nancy **often** goes to the zoo.
└─ (일반동사 앞) ┘

Go for it!

A. Look and write.

1. 100% → _____always_____

2. about 90% → _____

3. about 70% → _____

4. about 50% → _____

5. about 10% → _____

6. 0% → _____

B. Put the words in the right order.

1. make / I / some cookies / usually
   → *I usually make some cookies* _____.

2. They / to school / always / walk
   → _____.

3. She / watch / never / a horror movie
   → _____.

4. He / to the beach / go / often
   → _____.

C. Check(✓) the place for a frequency adverb.

1. She ⓐ goes ⓑ to ⓒ the church ⓓ on Sundays. (always)

2. Sunny ⓐ plays ⓑ volleyball. (never)

3. The student ⓐ was ⓑ late ⓒ for school. (usually)

4. We ⓐ get ⓑ up ⓒ early. (hardly)

5. The school bus ⓐ is ⓑ late ⓒ. (always)

6. Laura ⓐ is ⓑ at ⓒ home. (usually)

7. The ⓐ door ⓑ is ⓒ open. (seldom)

8. She ⓐ drinks ⓑ some coffee ⓒ at night. (sometimes)

D. Complete the sentences with a given adverb.

1.

   She smiles happily. (always)

   ➡ *She always smiles happily* _____.

2.

   My parents watch TV. (hardly)

   ➡ _____.

3.

   The man is busy. (usually)

   ➡ _____.

84

Grammar in Writing

A. Look at the chart and complete the sentences.

How does Tiffany get to school?				
	walk	take a bus	ride her bicycle	go by a car
always				
usually	1. √			
often		2 √		
sometimes			3. √	
seldom				
never				4. √

1. Tiffany _____ *usually walks to school* _____ .
2. Tiffany _____ .
3. Tiffany _____ .
4. Tiffany _____ .

B. Write the sentences with a *always*, *usually*, *sometimes* or *hardly*.

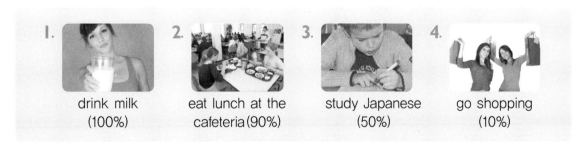

| 1. drink milk (100%) | 2. eat lunch at the cafeteria (90%) | 3. study Japanese (50%) | 4. go shopping (10%) |

1. She _____ *always drinks milk* _____ .
2. They _____ .
3. He _____ .
4. Susie and Kate _____ .

unit 3 Comparative

Grammar focus

The deer is **fast**.
The cheetah is fast**er than** the deer.

The MP3 player is **expensive**.
The iPhone is **more** expensive **than** the MP3 player.

1. 비교급이 뭐예요?

　두 가지의 비슷한 대상을 두고 서로를 비교하는 표현을 비교급이라고 해요. 〈비교급＋than〉의 형태로, '…보다 더 ~하다'라는 의미예요.

2. 비교급은 어떻게 만드나요?

　❶ 대부분의 형용사 끝에 -er을 붙여요. 당연히 -e로 끝나는 단어는 -r만 붙이면 돼요.

　　long – long**er**　　tall – tall**er**　　small – small**er**　　nice – nic**er**

　❷ 1음절의 단어가 〈단모음＋단자음〉으로 끝나는 단어는 마지막 자음을 하나 더 쓰고 -er을 붙여요.

　　hot – hot**ter**　　fat – fat**ter**　　big – big**ger**

　❸ y로 끝나는 단어는 끝의 y를 i로 고치고 -er을 붙여요.

　　happy – happ**ier**　　busy – bus**ier**　　heavy – heav**ier**

　❹ 형용사의 음절이 2음절 이상인 경우 형용사 앞에 more을 써서 〈more＋형용사＋than〉으로 써요.

　　beautiful – **more** beautiful　　expensive – **more** expensive
　　interesting – **more** interesting　　important – **more** important

Go for it!

A. Write the comparative form.

1. tall → *taller*

2. short → _____

3. big → _____

4. happy → _____

5. small → _____

6. large → _____

7. strong → _____

8. famous → _____

9. beautiful → _____

10. slow → _____

11. easy → _____

12. interesting → _____

13. expensive → _____

14. hot → _____

15. fat → _____

16. thin → _____

B. Look and write.

1.

   The earth is _____ *bigger than* _____ the moon.
   The moon is _____ *smaller than* _____ the earth.

   (big / small)

2. Tom is _____ Mary.
   Mary is _____ Tom.

   (tall / short)

3. The car is _____ the bicycle.
   The bicycle is _____ the car.

   (expensive / cheap)

C. Look and make comparisons.

1. *Spider Man* is ___*more interesting than*___ *Batman*. (interesting)

2. Love is _____ money. (important)

3. Math is _____ English. (difficult)

4. Thailand is _____ Korea. (hot)

5. The Amazon is _____ the Nile. (long)

6. Christina is _____ her grandmother. (young)

D. Look and write.

1.

Spring is warm.
Spring is ___*warmer than*___ winter.

2.

Steve is happy.
Steve is _____ Kathy.

3.

The basketball is big.
The basketball is _____ the soccer ball.

Grammar in Writing

A. Read and write the sentences with comparitives.

1. Sandra is 20 years old. Bob is 30. (old)
   → Bob ___*is older than Sandra*___ .

2. The CD player is 30 dollars. The MP3 player is 100. (expensive)
   → The MP3 player _____ .

3. London isn't very beautiful. Seoul is a beautiful city. (beautiful)
   → Seoul _____ .

4. English isn't difficult. Science is difficult. (difficult)
   → Science _____ .

B. Write comparisons in the blanks.

1. | Scott: 160cm
   | Jessica: 145cm

   Jessica is tall, but
   ___*Scott is taller than Jessica*___ .

2. | Kathy: 20kg
   | Jane: 18kg

   Kathy is thin, but
   _____ .

3. | *Harry Potter*: interesting
   | *Avatar*: more interesting

   Harry Potter is interesting, but
   _____ .

4. | Sunny: 60 years old
   | Steve: 70 years old

   Sunny is old, but
   _____ .

4 unit Superlative

Grammar focus

The giraffe is **the tallest** animal.　　　　It is **the longest** wall in the world.

1. 최상급이 뭐예요?

여러분들 모두 학교에서 제일 키가 크고 싶죠? 제일 공부 잘하고 싶죠? 이처럼 "누가 누가 제일 잘하나?"를 표현하는 것이 최상급이에요. 셋 이상의 사람이나 사물 중에서 '가장 ~한'이란 뜻으로 최고를 표현하는 방법이에요.

2. 최상급은 어떻게 만드나요?

최상급을 만드는 방법은 비교급하고 비슷해요. -er을 붙이는 것 대신에 -est를 붙이고, more 대신에 most를 붙여서 만들어요.

❶ 대부분의 형용사 끝에 -est를 붙여요. -e로 끝나면 -st만 붙이면 됩니다.

long ➡ the long**est**　　　　fast ➡ the fast**est**

large ➡ the larg**est**　　　　old ➡ the old**est**

❷ -y로 끝나는 단어는 y를 i로 고치고 -est를 붙여요.

happy ➡ the happ**iest**　　　　pretty ➡ the prett**iest**

❸ 〈단모음＋단자음〉으로 끝나는 단어는 마지막 철자를 한번 더 쓰고 -est를 붙여요.

big ➡ the big**gest**　　　　hot ➡ the hot**test**

❹ 2음절 이상의 소리가 나는 긴 단어는 단어 앞에 most를 붙여요.

famous ➡ the **most** famous　　　　difficult ➡ the **most** difficult

expensive ➡ the **most** expensive　　　　interesting ➡ the **most** interesting

❺ 불규칙변화

good ➡ better(비교급) ➡ the **best**(최상급)

bad ➡ worse(비교급) ➡ the **worst**(최상급)

Go for it!

A. Look and write.

	Comparative	Superlative
1. old	*older*	*oldest*
2. happy		
3. beautiful		
4. big		
5. expensive		
6. large		
7. hot		
8. cold		
9. good		
10. long		
11. difficult		
12. fast		
13. bad		
14. pretty		

B. Choose and write the superlative form.

hot	fast	high	large

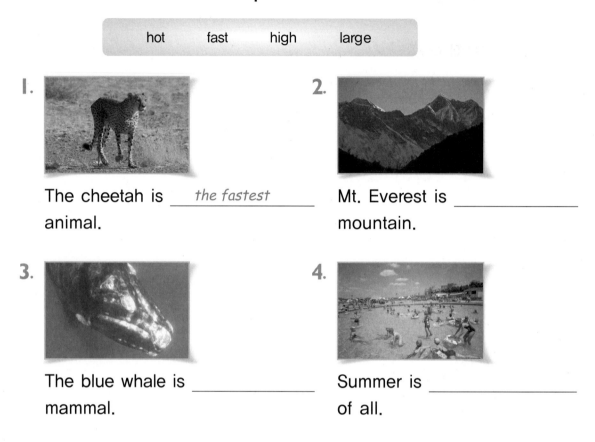

1. The cheetah is ___the fastest___ animal.

2. Mt. Everest is _____ mountain.

3. The blue whale is _____ mammal.

4. Summer is _____ of all.

C. Complete the sentences using the superlative form.

1. Seoul is ___the largest city___ in Korea.
   (city / large)

2. Mississippi is _____ in the USA.
   (river / long)

3. Russia is _____ in the world.
   (country / large)

4. February is _____ of the year.
   (month / short)

5. Rattle-snake is _____ in the world.
   (animal / dangerous)

Grammar in Writing

A. Compare the girls and complete the sentences.

tall & short
• Sunny: 170cm
• Kelly: 165cm
• Susan: 160cm

1. Sunny is _____taller_____ _____than_____ Kelly. (Comparative)

2. Susan is _____ _____ Kelly. (Comparative)

3. Sunny is _____ _____ of the three. (Superlative)

4. Susan is _____ _____ of the three. (Superlative)

B. Complete the dialogues.

1. A: What is the most beautiful flower?
   B: _The rose is the most beautiful flower_____. (rose)

2. A: Who is the happiest woman in the world?
   B: _____. (Jane)

3. A: Which is the highest mountain in the world?
   B: _____. (Mt. Everest)

4. A: Which is the longest river in the world?
   B: _____. (the Nile)

5. A: What is the largest mammal in the world?
   B: _____. (the blue whale)

Chapter 6
Helping Verbs & Tenses

Grammar focus

She's sleepy.
She **should** take a nap.

He has a toothache.
He **must** see a dentist.
He **mustn't** eat lots of sweets.

1. should는 언제 쓰는 건가요?

조동사 should는 우리말로 '~하는 게 좋겠다, ~하는 게 좋은 생각이다'라는 의미예요. 부정문은 조동사(should) 뒤에 not을 붙이고 '~하지 않는 게 좋겠다'의 뜻을 나타내요.

2. must는 언제 쓰는 건가요?

조동사 must는 우리말 '~해야 한다'의 뜻으로 어떤 일을 꼭 하라고 하는 강한 어조가 담겨 있어요. must의 부정문은 must 뒤에 not을 붙여, '~해서는 안 된다'라는 강한 금지를 나타내요.

should(it's a good idea to do something)	must(very important or necessary)
should + Ⓥ should not(shouldn't) + Ⓥ	must + Ⓥ must not(mustn't) + Ⓥ
Should I be quiet in the library? – Yes, you should. / No, you shouldn't.	Must Tom do his homework? – Yes, he must. / No, he mustn't.

Usage

She has a cold.
She **should** see a doctor.

You **must** be quiet in class.
You **must** listen to the teacher.

Go for it!

A. Complete the sentences with *must* or *mustn't*.

1.

You ___must___ stop.

2.

You _____ smoke here.

3.

You _____ turn left.

4.

You _____ swim here.

B. Choose and write with *should* or *shouldn't*.

| speak in class | eat more | go to bed early | watch TV |

1.

You ___should eat more___.

2.

Alice _____
so much.

3.

Jessica _____.

4.

You _____.

C. Put the words in the right order.

I. mustn't / take pictures / you

   ➡ *You mustn't take pictures* _____.

2. should / they / their teeth / brush

   ➡ _____.

3. she / home late / shouldn't / come

   ➡ _____.

4. we / to our teacher / listen / should

   ➡ _____.

5. eat / sweets / he / mustn't

   ➡ _____.

D. Complete the sentences with *must* or *mustn't*.

> Welcome to the Art Museum!
> Please follow the rules.
>
> I. You _____*must*_____ buy a ticket.
>
> 2. You _____ eat or drink in the museum.
>
> 3. You _____ smoke in the museum.
>
> 4. You _____ be quiet in the museum.
>
> 5. You _____ take pictures.
>
> 6. You _____ touch the paintings.

Grammar in Writing

A. Rewrite the sentences with *must* or *mustn't*.

1. Do exercise for your health.
   → You ____*must exercise for your health*____ .

2. Don't eat the hamburger.
   → You _____ .

3. Don't be late for class.
   → You _____ .

4. Don't park here.
   → You _____ .

5. Go to bed early.
   → You _____ .

B. Rewrite the sentences with *should* or *shouldn't*.

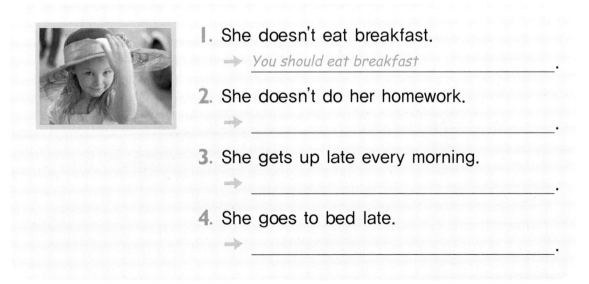

1. She doesn't eat breakfast.
   → *You should eat breakfast* _____ .

2. She doesn't do her homework.
   → _____ .

3. She gets up late every morning.
   → _____ .

4. She goes to bed late.
   → _____ .

unit 2 Ⓥ ~ & Let's + Ⓥ ~

Grammar focus

Don't sleep in the classroom.　　　**Let's** take a picture.

1. 명령문이 뭐예요?

상대방에게 '~해라'라고 명령하는 말을 명령문이라고 해요. 상대방(you)에게 말하는 것이므로 주어인 you를 생략하고, 문장 맨 앞을 동사원형으로 시작해요. '~하지 마라'라는 뜻의 부정명령문은 동사원형 앞에 Don't를 써주면 돼요.

Postitive(긍정)	Negative(부정)
Open the door. Be careful.	Don't drink a lot of coffee. Don't be afraid of the dog.

2. 제안문이 뭐예요?

제안문은 '나'를 포함한 상대방과 주변 사람에게 '우리 ~하자'라고 제안하는 말이에요. 동사원형 앞에 Let's를 써서 나타내고 '(우리)~하지 말자'라는 부정문을 만들 때는 Let's 뒤에 not을 붙이면 돼요. Let's는 〈Let+us〉의 줄임말이랍니다.

Let's + Ⓥ	Let's not + Ⓥ
Let's go shopping.	Let's not watch TV.

Usage

Don't eat sweets.　　　It's sunny.
Brush your teeth.　　　**Let's** walk to school.

Go for it!

A. Circle the correct word.

1.

   (Don't run / Run) in the hallway.

2.

   (Speak / Don't speak) loudly.

3.

   (Let's / Don't) eat pizza.

4.

   (Let's / Let's not) be late for school.

5.

   (Let's / Don't) eat chocolate so much.

6.

   It's cold. (Let's close / Open) the window.

B. Complete the sentence with *Let's* or *Let's not.*

not make	go	not watch	eat	not go	make

1. It's time to have lunch. _____*Let's eat*_____ lunch.

2. I have tickets for the show. _____ to the museum.

3. We have a lot of homework. _____ TV.

4. The baby is sleeping now. _____ a noise.

5. It's rainy outside. _____ out today.

6. I am so hungry. _____ some food.

C. Circle the correct word.

1. Let's (goes / go) to the amusement park.

2. (Opens / Open) the door.

3. Don't (climbed / climb) the tree.

4. Let's not (play / played) volleyball.

5. (Do / Did) your homework.

6. Let's not (ate / eat) pizza tonight.

Grammar in Writing

A. Change the sentences with *Let's*.

1. We should go to a movie tonight.
   → *Let's go to a movie tonight* _____ .

2. We should go on a picnic this Sunday.
   → _____ .

3. We should wash our hands before dinner.
   → _____ .

4. We should go home and study hard.
   → _____ .

5. We should brush our teeth after meal.
   → _____ .

B. Look and write.

Should I wait for you?	→ No, don't wait for me.
Should we go to the beach?	→ No, let's not go to the beach.

1. Should we go to the seafood restaurant?
   → No, _____ .

2. Should I take my umbrella?
   → No, _____ .

3. Should we study English together?
   → No, _____ .

4. Should I listen to music?
   → No, _____ .

5. Should we stay at home?
   → No, _____ .

Present Continuous Ⅱ

Grammar focus

A: What **are** you **doing** tonight?
B: I**'m visiting** my grandma.

A: When **is** John **leaving** here?
B: He**'s leaving** for Australia next week.

1. 현재진행형이 미래를 나타낼 수 있나요?

어떤 일을 하기로 미리 정해진 경우, 현재진행형이 미래를 나타낼 수 있어요. 일상회화에서 진행형을 써서 미래를 나타내는 표현을 자주 써요.

2. be going to와 같은 뜻인가요?

이미 정해진 계획과 일정에만 현재 진행형과 be going to가 서로 같은 의미로 사용 돼요. 단순히 미래를 예상하는 일에는 현재 진행형을 쓰지 않고, will 또는 be going to를 써야 해요.

am / is / are + ⓥ-ing		be going to + ⓥ-ing
Jane is leaving at 8:00 tomorrow. What are you doing tonight?	=	Jane is going to leave at 8:00 tomorrow. What are you going to do tonight?

Usage

A: What **are** you **doing** tonight?
B: We**'re watching** a movie.

A: What **are** Linda **doing** this Sunday?
B: She**'s cleaning** her bedroom.

Go for it!

A. Read and complete the answers.

1.

   Q: What is Kathy doing this Saturday?
   A: She _____*is playing tennis*_____.
   (play tennis)

2.

   Q: What is Nancy doing this Saturday?
   A: She _____.
   (listen to music)

3.

   Q: What is Tom doing this Saturday?
   A: He _____.
   (travel to Singapore)

4.

   Q: What are they doing this Saturday?
   A: They _____.
   (go to the movie theater)

5.

   Q: What are you doing this Saturday?
   A: I _____.
   (study Korean)

B. Read and change the sentences.

1. Laura is leaving for her trip next week.
   → Laura _____ *is going to leave for her trip next week* _____.

2. We are driving to Toronto next week.
   → We _____.

3. Peter is riding his skateboard next week.
   → Peter _____.

4. Jane is travelling to Japan next week.
   → Jane _____.

5. Josephine is working in the office next week.
   → Josephine _____.

C. Look and write.

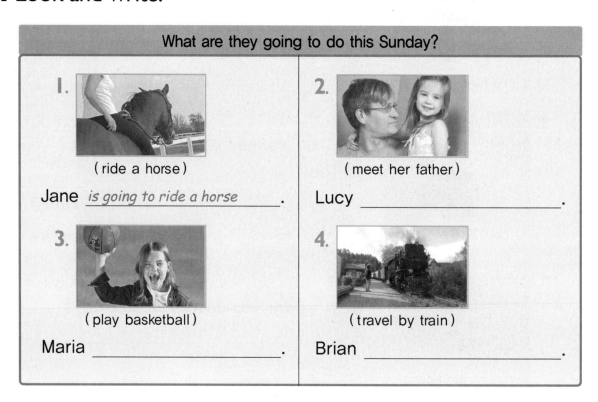

What are they going to do this Sunday?

1. (ride a horse)
   Jane *is going to ride a horse* .

2. (meet her father)
   Lucy _____.

3. (play basketball)
   Maria _____.

4. (travel by train)
   Brian _____.

Grammar in Writing

A. Look and make sentences.

My Summer Vacation Plan
1. visit grandparents
2. travel to Paris
3. go to a museum
4. go to the beach
5. meet David
6. run the Marathon

1. *I am visiting grandparents* _____ .

2. _____ .

3. _____ .

4. _____ .

5. _____ .

6. _____ .

B. Look and answer the questions.

1.
(play tennis with Tom)

Q: Is she playing soccer next Monday?
A: No, she isn't.
　　She is playing tennis with Tom _____ .

2.
(read a book)

Q: Is your mom watching TV tonight?
A: No, she isn't.
　　_____ .

3.
(paint the house)

Q: Is Lucy going to the concert next week?
A: No, she isn't.
　　_____ .

Past Continuous II

They **were** hav**ing** dinner at 8:00 yesterday.

They **weren't** watch**ing** TV.

Q: **Were** they hav**ing** dinner?

A: **Yes**, they **were**. / **No**, they **weren't**.

1. 과거진행형의 부정문은 어떻게 만들어요?

과거진행형의 부정문을 만들 때는 be동사 was, were 바로 뒤에 not을 붙여주면 돼요. 우리말로 '~하고 있지 않았(었)다'의 뜻이 돼요.

2. 의문문은 어떻게 만드나요?

과거진행형의 의문문을 만들 때는 be동사(was, were)를 문장 맨 앞으로 보내고 물음표(?)를 써주면 돼요. 그리고 was, were를 이용해서 답하면 돼요.

Subject + was(were) + not + Ⓥ-ing	Was(Were) + subject + Ⓥ-ing ?
I / She / He / It wasn't working.	Was [I / she / he / it] sleeping? Were [you / we / they] sleeping?
You / We / They weren't working.	Yes, [I / she / he / it] was. No, [you / we / they] weren't.

Usage

The students **weren't** study**ing**.
They were walking.

Q: **Was** she sleep**ing** at 10:00 last night?
A: **No**, she **wasn't**.
    She was talking on the phone.

Go for it!

A. Match and write.

1. listen

She ___wasn't___ studying.
She ___was___ ___listening___ to music.

2. read

He _____ driving a car.
He _____ _____ a newspaper.

3. brush

You _____ studying.
You _____ _____ your teeth.

4. watch

They _____ singing.
They _____ _____ TV.

B. Look and complete the questions.

1.

(sleep)
Q: ___Was___ she
___sleeping___ ?
A: Yes, she was.

2.

(jog)
Q: _____ you
_____ ?
A: Yes, I was.

3.
(swim)
Q: _____ Tom
_____ ?
A: Yes, he was.

C. Answer the questions.

1.

Q: Were they walking in the park?
A: ___Yes___ , _____they were_____ .

2.

Q: Were the girls studying in the library?
A: _____ , _____ .

3.

Q: Was Lucy driving a car?
A: _____ , _____ .

4.

Q: Were you having dinner?
A: _____ , _____ .

D. Complete the questions and answers.

1. ___Was___ Sunny drinking coffee?   → Yes, ___she was___ .

2. _____ they working?   → No, _____ .

3. _____ he waiting for a bus?   → Yes, _____ .

4. _____ Sunny taking off her socks?   → No, _____ .

5. _____ the girls dancing on the stage?   → Yes, _____ .

6. _____ she riding her bicycle?   → No, _____ .

Grammar in Writing

A. Complete the sentences.

1. sleep(X) / clean(O)
2. skate(X) / eat(O)
3. drink(X) / wash(O)

1. My mom ___*wasn't sleeping*___ .
   My mom ___*was cleaning*___ the floor.

2. Jane and Susie _____ .
   Jane and Susie _____ ice cream.

3. They _____ juice.
   They _____ the car.

B. Look at the pictures. Write questions and answers.

1. he / wash the dishes / No / water the garden
   Q: *Was he washing the dishes* ?
   A: *No, he wasn't. He was watering the garden* .

2. the students / listen to music / No / study
   Q: _____ ?
   A: _____ .

3. Steve / talk on the phone / No / brush his teeth
   Q: _____ ?
   A: _____ .